SHOW WHAT YOU KNOW!

Taking and Organizing Notes

by Ellen Range

LIGHTBOX
openlightbox.com

LIGHTBOX

Go to
www.openlightbox.com
and enter this book's
unique code.

ACCESS CODE

LBXM6677

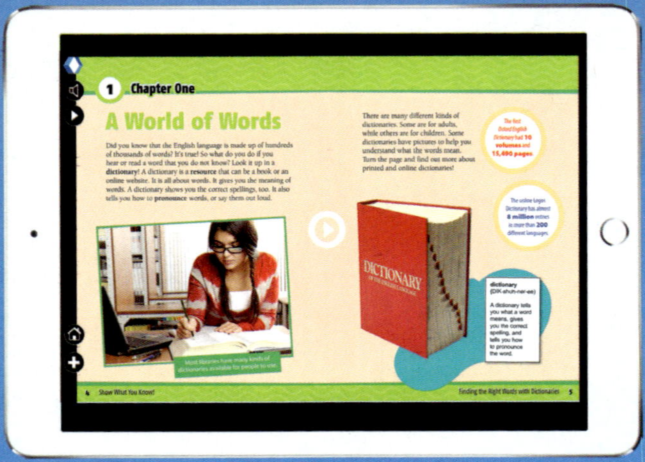

Lightbox is an all-inclusive digital solution for the teaching and learning of curriculum topics in an original, groundbreaking way. Lightbox is based on National Curriculum Standards.

STANDARD FEATURES OF LIGHTBOX

AUDIO High-quality narration using text-to-speech system

ACTIVITIES Printable PDFs that can be emailed and graded

SLIDESHOWS Pictorial overviews of key concepts

VIDEOS Embedded high-definition video clips

WEBLINKS Curated links to external, child-safe resources

TRANSPARENCIES Step-by-step layering of maps, diagrams, charts, and timelines

INTERACTIVE MAPS Interactive maps and aerial satellite imagery

QUIZZES Ten multiple choice questions that are automatically graded and emailed for teacher assessment

KEY WORDS Matching key concepts to their definitions

Taking and Organizing Notes

1 Chapter One

What Is Note Taking?

Have you ever forgotten something important? Maybe you forgot to bring your sneakers to school on gym day. Or perhaps you forgot when your friend's birthday party was supposed to start. Taking notes is one way to avoid forgetting things. Notes are short messages. You don't need to write whole sentences in notes. You just need to write the important parts. For example, a note probably wouldn't say, "Tomorrow is gym day. Don't forget to bring your sneakers!" It would say "sneakers tomorrow" or even just "sneakers."

You can also use notes to remember information that you read about. Sometimes your reading leads you to ideas you want to think about later. You may also make **predictions** about what will happen next. However, you might forget about these ideas as you keep reading. Taking notes as you read is a great way to remember your thoughts. You can look over your notes later and remember what you were thinking about as you read.

The world's **longest** pencil is **3,582 feet** (1,092 meters) long.

The average middle school student can write about **60 letters per minute**.

Sometimes a note can be a sketch instead of words.

Taking notes is a little like making a sandwich. You have to gather the bread and ingredients first. Then you arrange them in the right order to make a tasty snack. When taking notes, you have to gather the information first. Then you put it together in a way that makes sense to you. There are many ways to take notes. In this book, we'll look at some note-taking **strategies**.

Just like when making a sandwich, notes should be organized in a logical order.

Try This

Notes should use as few words as possible. For example, if a book says, "Most mice eat seeds or grass," you might make a note that reads, "Food = seeds, grass." Writing just the important words on your note saves you time! Try turning the following sentences into short notes.

1. The United States of America is made up of 50 individual states.

2. The basketball game will begin at 7:00 PM.

3. The first working airplane was built and tested by brothers Orville and Wilbur Wright in 1903.

History of Note Taking

3200 BC Ancient **Sumerians** create the oldest known examples of note taking by pressing a plant stem into clay tablets.

1000 BC The Greeks develop an alphabet, which leads to many of the alphabets used around the world today.

1800 BC The first known alphabet is used in ancient Egypt.

About 1760 Scientist Carl Linnaeus first uses note cards to keep track of information on plants, animals, and minerals.

1874 The first typewriters, invented by American Christopher Latham Sholes, are sold. They begin to replace pens and paper for writing and note taking.

1977 January 23 becomes National Handwriting Day in the United States. It is the birthday of John Hancock, who is famous for his signature on the U.S. Declaration of Independence.

2017 Vishwendra Singh of India wins the World Handwriting Contest. The annual competition is open to writers and note takers of all ages.

Mapping Note Taking

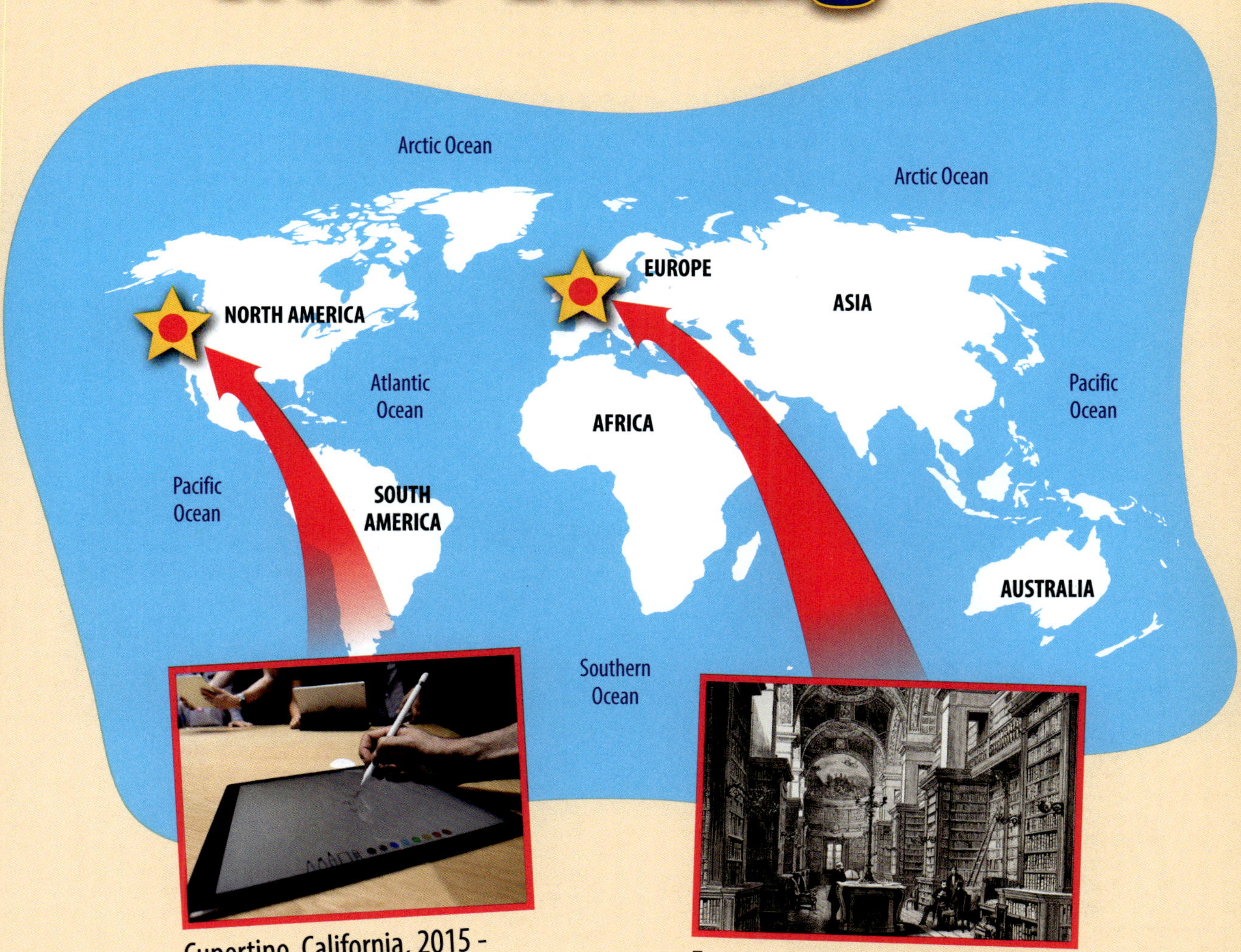

Cupertino, California, 2015 - Tech company Apple releases the Apple Pencil, a pencil-like tool that can be used to take notes with an iPad tablet.

France, 1791 - Rather than using a notebook, librarians begin using note cards to keep track of their books. At first, they write the information on the backs of playing cards.

2 Chapter Two

Sticky Notes

Using sticky notes is one popular tool to keep track of information. As you read, you may find words that seem important. You might read things that you want to remember later. You might even have questions about something in the book. Sticky notes give you a place to write down those ideas or questions. You can stick them on the side of the page you are reading. You can also keep them in a folder. As you keep reading, you may find that the book answers a question you had earlier. You can go back to your sticky notes and write down answers as you find them.

What should you write down? Think about the main idea of the book and other information that seems important. Then ask yourself two questions: (1) What did I learn from what I read? and (2) What do I need to remember? Take notes when you find information that could answer these questions. Use a new sticky note for each new idea.

Sticky notes come in many colors. Ella likes to use different colors for different kinds of notes. This helps her organize her information. She uses green notes for information about important people. Pink notes are used for dates. Blue notes mark new **vocabulary** words. When she looks at her notes later, the colors make it easy to find different kinds of information.

Write notes as you read. You may forget things if you wait until later.

Try This

Visit the library and check out a book about an animal. Then grab a pencil and some sticky notes. Read your book and look closely for interesting facts. Write each piece of information down on a new sticky note. Stick each note along the edge of the page where you found the information. You can also write down questions you have as you read. For example, a book about cats might make you wonder, "How do cats always land on their feet?"

Look over your notes once you have finished the book. Did your questions get answered? How did your notes help you keep track of useful information?

3 Chapter Three

Tables

Creating a table is another good strategy for note taking. Tables organize your information into **columns** and **rows**. They can make it easier to see what information you have found and what you still need to learn.

Mia's teacher has asked her to research a famous person, Rosa Parks. Mia needs to find out when Parks was born, where she lived, and what made her famous. A table is a great way to organize this information.

To make a table, Mia draws a box on a piece of paper. Then she draws some lines across to make rows. She draws lines up and down to make columns. Next, she labels the top of the table "Rosa Parks." In the first column, Mia writes the questions that her teacher assigned. She puts one question in each box of the column. Now she knows what to look for as she researches. Next to each question, Mia has a box for writing the answer!

Mia writes down only the most useful information she finds. If she tried to write down everything, it would be harder to find what she is looking for later. Her hand would get tired, too!

Rosa Parks

When was she born?	
Where did she live?	
What made her famous?	

Try This

Not all information comes from books. You can learn a lot just by talking to people! An interview is a time for you to ask someone questions. Try using a table to organize information for an interview.

An interview gives you a chance to learn about people's experiences.

1. Find someone who is willing to talk with you. This could be a family member or a friend.

2. In one column of your table, write down five things you want to know about that person. Maybe you want to ask about the person's favorite food or hobbies.

3. Ask the person each question.

4. Write down the answers in the second column of your table. Remember to keep your notes short and simple.

5. When you are done asking questions, thank the person for letting you conduct the interview.

4 Chapter Four

Visual Note Taking

We have learned that there are many ways to take notes. You can mark important ideas or keep track of questions with sticky notes. You can also use tables to arrange your notes. Making sketches or drawings is another way to get ideas on paper. You can draw pictures to add to your writing, make a map, or create a flowchart. Flowcharts use arrows, words, and images to show the steps of a process. Imagine that your teacher has explained how tadpoles grow into frogs. A flowchart with pictures and arrows can help you see this process more clearly.

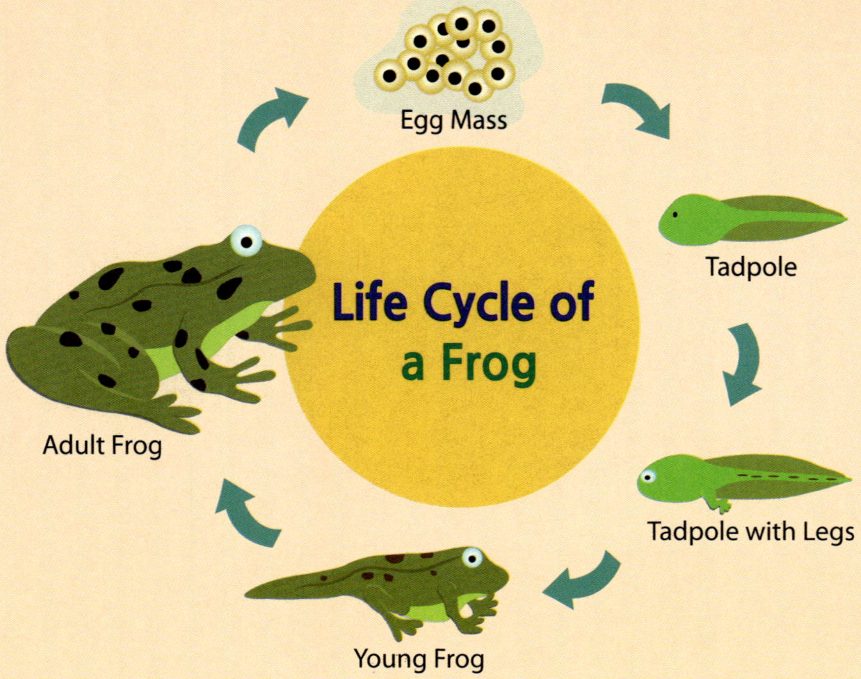

Jeremy and his family are taking a trip to the state of Michigan. They want to visit some state parks along their route. Jeremy labels all the parks they will be driving by on a map of Michigan. The labeled map shows them how many parks there are. It also shows how far apart the parks are.

Sometimes you might want to compare two or more things. Try using a **Venn diagram** to organize this information. A Venn diagram is a drawing of circles that **overlap**. On a sheet of unlined paper, draw two circles. Label each circle with the name of one of the things you are comparing. Put things that are only true for one topic in the big part of the circle. In the overlapping part, write down things that the topics have in common.

Annie wants to learn about the planet Venus. She is curious how Venus is like and unlike Earth. She makes a Venn diagram to display her comparisons. She labels one big circle "Venus" and the other "Earth." She includes weather, color, and size in her diagram. Where the circles overlap, she writes things that the planets have in common. Things they don't have in common stay in the separate bigger circles.

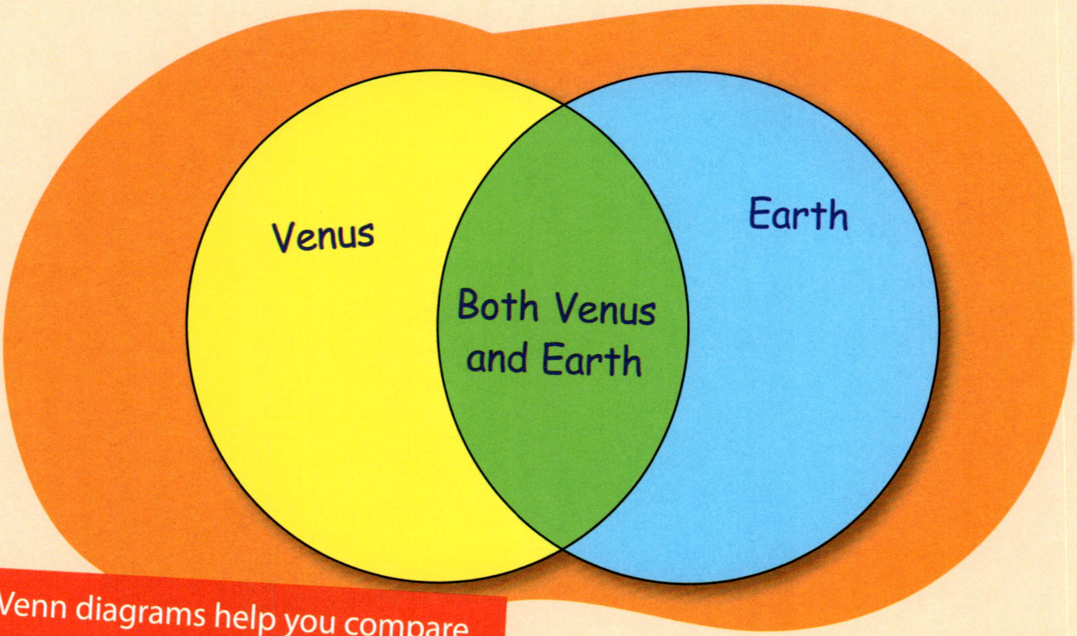

Venn diagrams help you compare two or more things, such as planets.

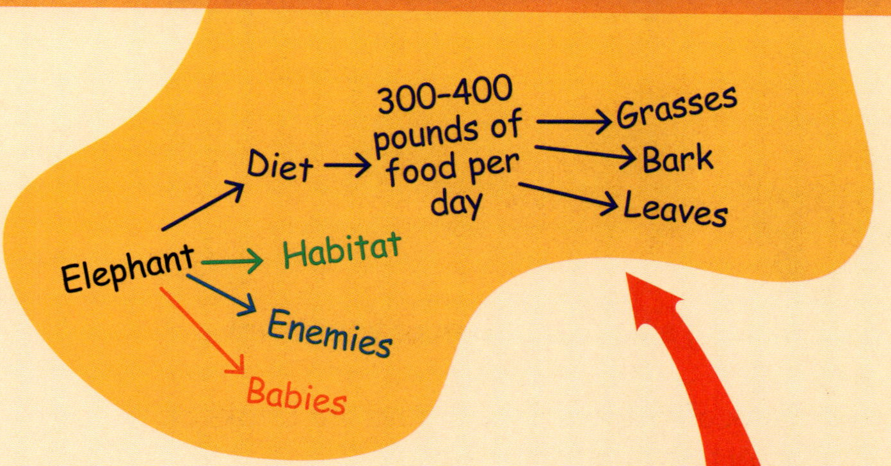

Another type of visual note is the web-shaped drawing. These drawings are often called mind maps, word webs, or graphic organizers. Gabe uses a web-shaped drawing to learn about elephants. He writes his topic, elephant, in the middle. Then he draws lines outward and puts important ideas about the animal at the end of each line. He includes information about the animal's diet, habitat, enemies, and babies. As he learns more about each of these smaller topics, he draws more lines going outward.

Remember that note taking is personal. The method that works best for you may not work for your friend. Also, the same method may not work for every task. Don't be afraid to try out different note-taking strategies. You are on your way to becoming a note-taking expert!

Web-shaped drawings can take any shape.

Math expert **John Venn** invented Venn diagrams in the **1880s**.

People have been making **mind maps** and web-shaped drawings since about **300 AD**.

Try This

Try making a Venn diagram of your own!

- Think about two of your favorite books or stories. Draw two circles that overlap.
- In one circle of your diagram, write down your favorite things about Book #1.
- In the other circle, write down your favorite things about Book #2.
- In the overlapping section, write down everything you can think of that relates to both books. Do they both have happy endings? Can you read all of the words in both books without help? Are both books about a dog?
- When you're finished, look at the information you have gathered. What has this Venn diagram taught you about your favorite books? This information could help you find new books to read!

Quiz

1
Do you need to write whole sentences when taking notes?

2
When taking notes, what do you have to do first?

3
Should notes include as many or as few words as possible?

4
How do tables organize information?

5
Around 1760, what scientist used note cards to keep track of things?

6
Whose birthday is on January 23, National Handwriting Day?

7
What do flowcharts use to show the steps of a process?

8
What is an interview?

9
How can you use sketches or drawings to take notes?

10
What is a Venn diagram?

Answers: 1. No **2.** Gather the information **3.** As few words as possible **4.** In columns and rows **5.** Carl Linnaeus **6.** John Hancock **7.** Arrows, words, and images **8.** A time for you to ask someone questions. **9.** You can draw pictures, make a map, or create a flowchart **10.** A drawing of circles that overlap

Key Words

columns: series of numbers or words that run up and down in a chart or table

overlap: to extend over or partly cover something

predictions: things you think will happen in the future

rows: series of numbers or words that run side to side in a chart or table

strategies: plans for achieving a goal

Sumerians: ancient people who lived in what is now Iraq from about 4000 to 2000 BC

Venn diagram: a graph that organizes information using overlapping circles

vocabulary: all the words that a person can use and understand

Index

LIGHTBOX

SUPPLEMENTARY RESOURCES

Click on the plus icon ⊕ found in the bottom left corner of each spread to open additional teacher resources.

- Download and print the book's quizzes and activities
- Access curriculum correlations
- Explore additional web applications that enhance the Lightbox experience

LIGHTBOX DIGITAL TITLES
Packed full of integrated media

VIDEOS

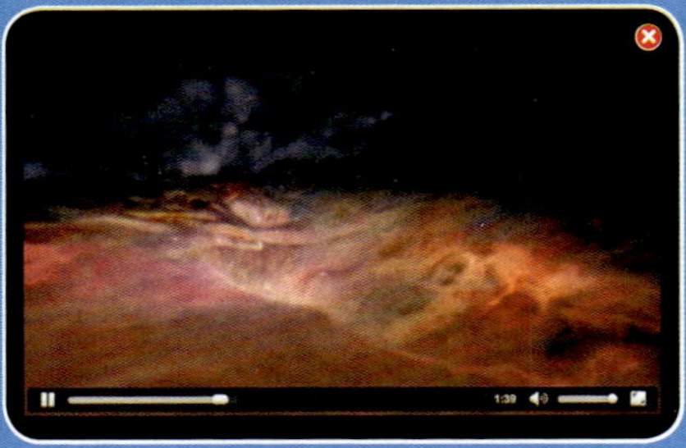

INTERACTIVE MAPS

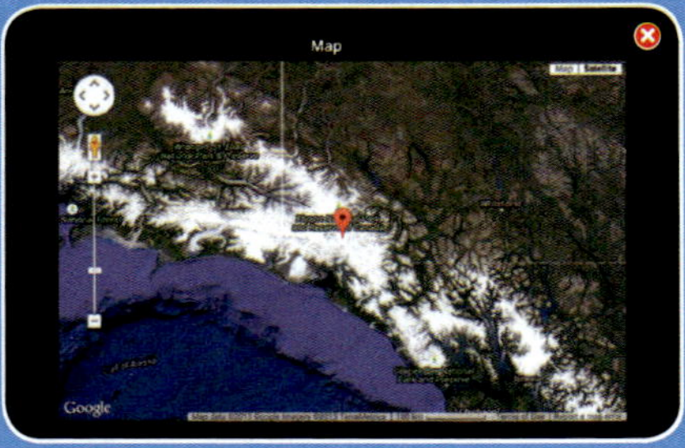

WEBLINKS

SLIDESHOWS

QUIZZES

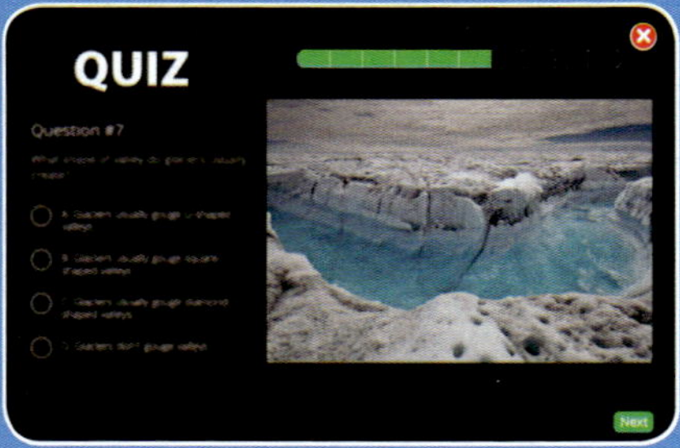

OPTIMIZED FOR

- ✔ TABLETS
- ✔ WHITEBOARDS
- ✔ COMPUTERS
- ✔ AND MUCH MORE!

Published by Smartbook Media Inc. 350 5th Avenue, 59th Floor New York, NY 10118
Website: www.openlightbox.com

First published by Cherry Lake Publishing in 2013

Library of Congress Control Number: 2018941478

ISBN 978-1-5105-3975-4 (hardcover)
ISBN 978-1-5105-3976-1 (multi-user eBook)

Printed in Brainerd, Minnesota, United States
1 2 3 4 5 6 7 8 9 0 22 21 20 19 18

062018
120517

Project Coordinator Heather Kissock
Designer Nick Newton

Photo Credits
Every reasonable effort has been made to trace ownership and to obtain permission to reprint copyright material. The publisher would be pleased to have any errors or omissions brought to its attention so that they may be corrected in subsequent printings.

The publisher acknowledges Getty Images, Shutterstock, and Alamy as its primary image suppliers for this title.